Computer Crazy

Computer Crazy

by Daniel Le Noury

Captions translated and adapted by Paul Panish

Berkeley • Paris • Düsseldorf

This book is part of the SYBEX Popular Series
developed by Doug Mosher, Division Manager.

Cover Art by Daniel Le Noury
Design by Ingrid Owen
Series Editor for Illustrated Books: Barbara Gordon
Senior Production Editor: Karl Ray

Library of Congress Card Number: 84-50034
ISBN 0-89588-173-X
Printed in the United States of America
10 9 8 7 6 5 4 3 2 1

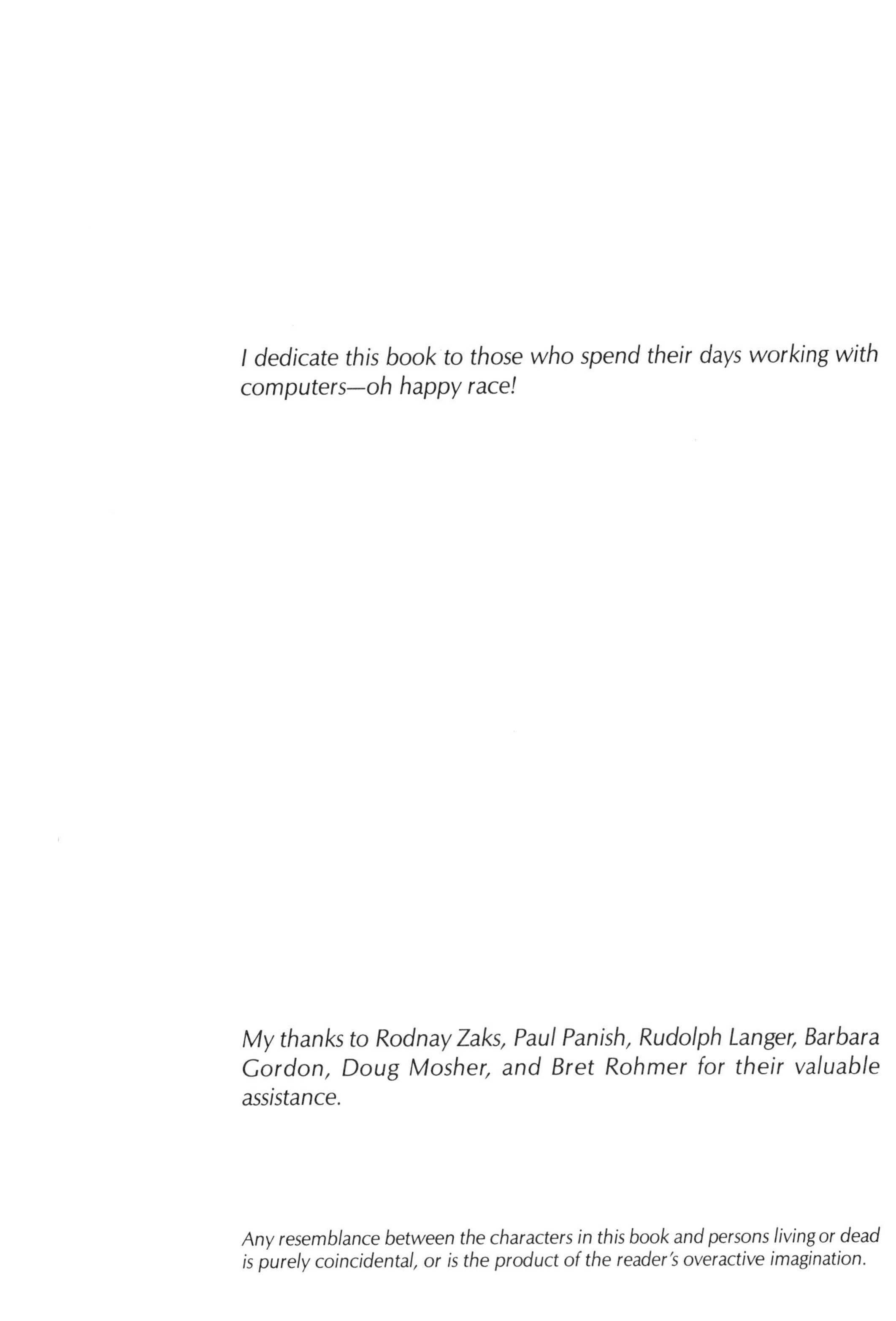

I dedicate this book to those who spend their days working with computers—oh happy race!

My thanks to Rodnay Zaks, Paul Panish, Rudolph Langer, Barbara Gordon, Doug Mosher, and Bret Rohmer for their valuable assistance.

Any resemblance between the characters in this book and persons living or dead is purely coincidental, or is the product of the reader's overactive imagination.

YOUR
FLY
IS
OPEN
Lenoury

I feel more and more dominated by my microoo01001o1000111110 . . .

lenoury

Am I to understand that your computer says we're off the coast of Kansas? . . .

*But what will we **do** with ourselves when computers do all the work?*

Probably an idol worshipped by some lost civilization . . .

Now all we have to do is miniaturize ***ourselves!***

Check it! Check it! There's ***gotta*** *be a bug! . . .*

Waddaya mean, user error!?

Doctor, it's my wife here—she's convinced she's an Apple . . .

Just like they said, my computer really liberated me . . .

I forgot to type "Find the ***constellation*** *big bear" . . .*

Don't ever try to fake the password with this one . . .

It says we'll never find oil around here . . .

So ***that's*** *interactive software! . . .*

Keep trying, Lefty . . . we still have exactly seven minutes 'till the cops get here! . . .

Don't let them see what you can do with that or it's 8 hours a day in the office! . . .

It's my kid's new Star Wars game! . . .

DO YOU KNOW WHAT TIME IT IS!? WHERE HAVE YOU BEEN!? DID YOU BRING THE BATTERIES FOR ME? I CAN'T JUST SIT HERE DOING SQUARE ROOTS ALL NIGHT! NOW LET ME TELL YOU . . . .

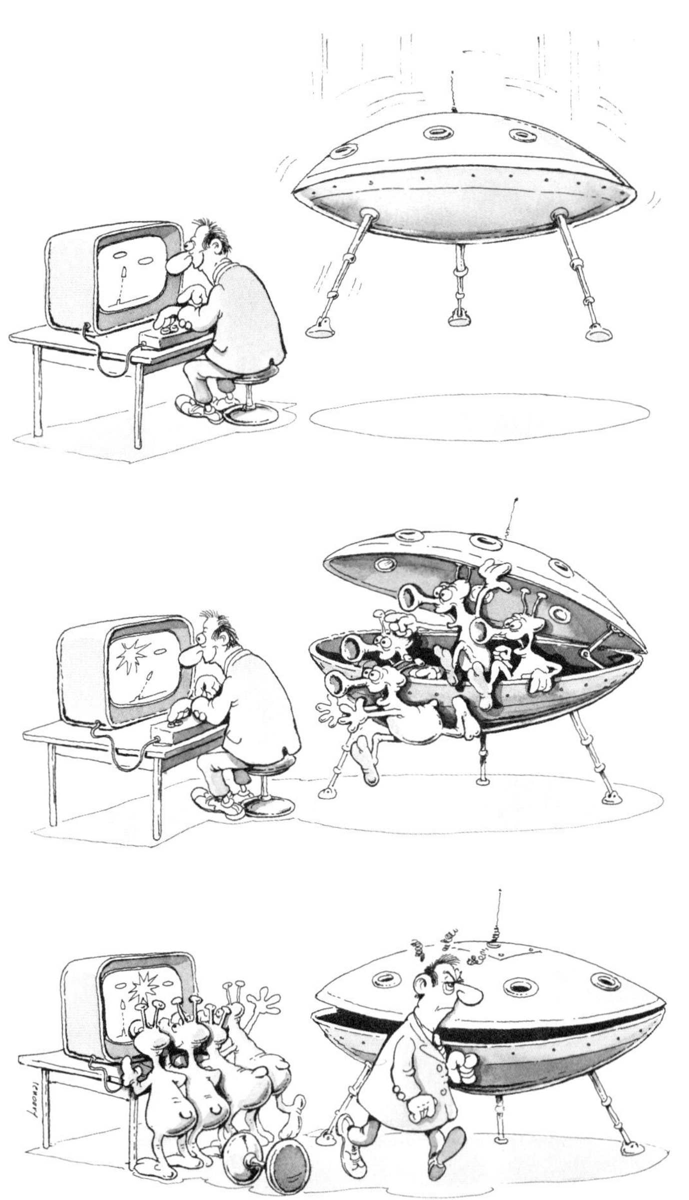

We ***never*** *lost that 25 million, Harry! It was just a glitch in the computer printout!*

Y'see? I still got the ol' sex appeal goin' for me!

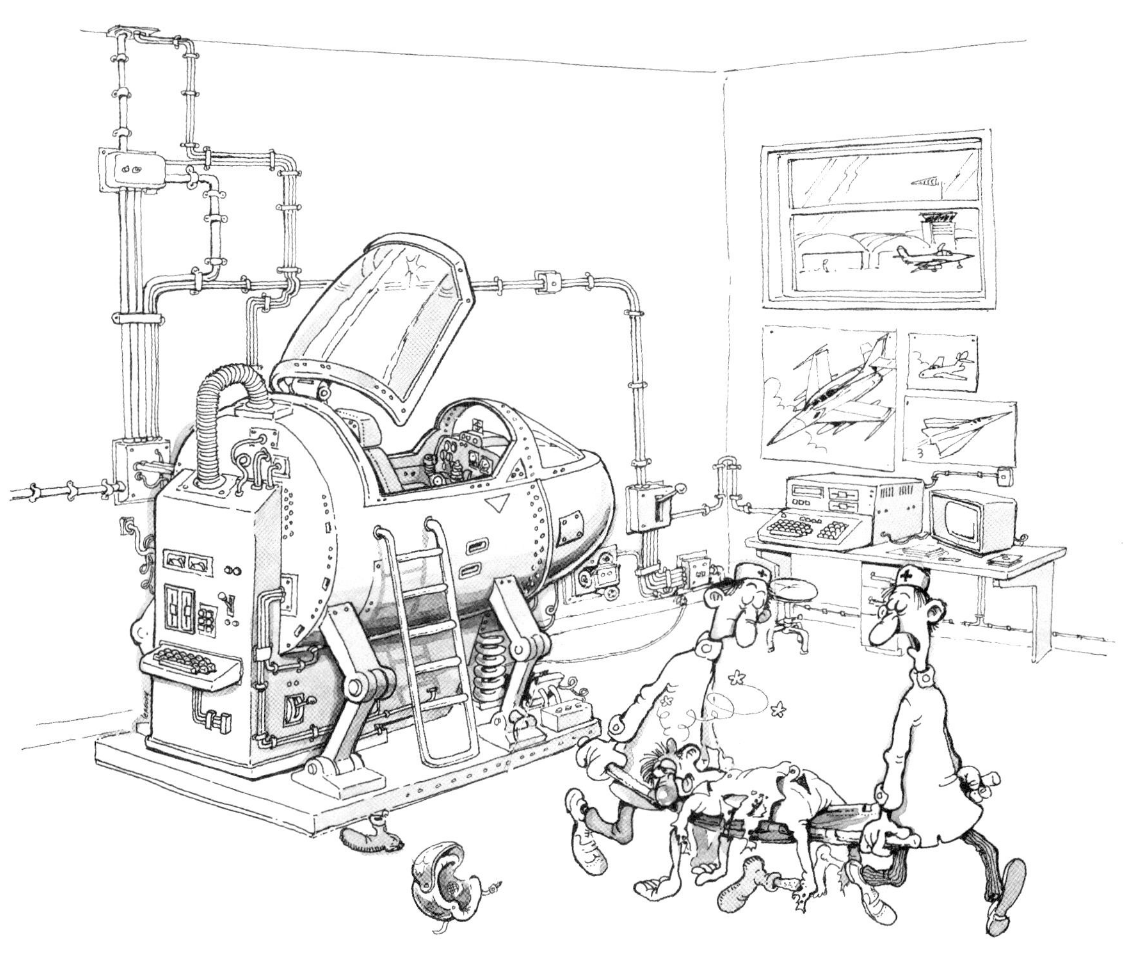

These computerized flight simulators are just a bit too realistic—
especially for crash landings . . .

What're your 64 kilobytes of memory compared to even the smallest galaxy, with its millions of solar systems and tens of millions of suns? . . .

Just a little bug in the guidance program, Sarge!

I think it needs the ol' shock treatment!

*They were right! Computers **do** make it much easier to take inventory.*

Thanks, but I've got all the memory I need.

I don't know about our position, but the stock market is due for an upswing.

. . . then use the AØ line for internal register selection, connect the other three signals to the control bus, and scrape the sheep crap off your boots.

The computer-generated strategy? PRAY.

The Space Invaders! . . . They've blown up my flagship!

START
KEYSTROKE
SIGNAL PLAYER
COUNTER
DELAY A BIT
DURAT
X=3
DELAY
PLAY LOW TONE
COUNTER
PLAY SEQUENCE
LED POINTER
SPIN
DONE RET
SCORE
FILL CON
KEYNUMBER
X=X-1
LED POINTER
lenoury

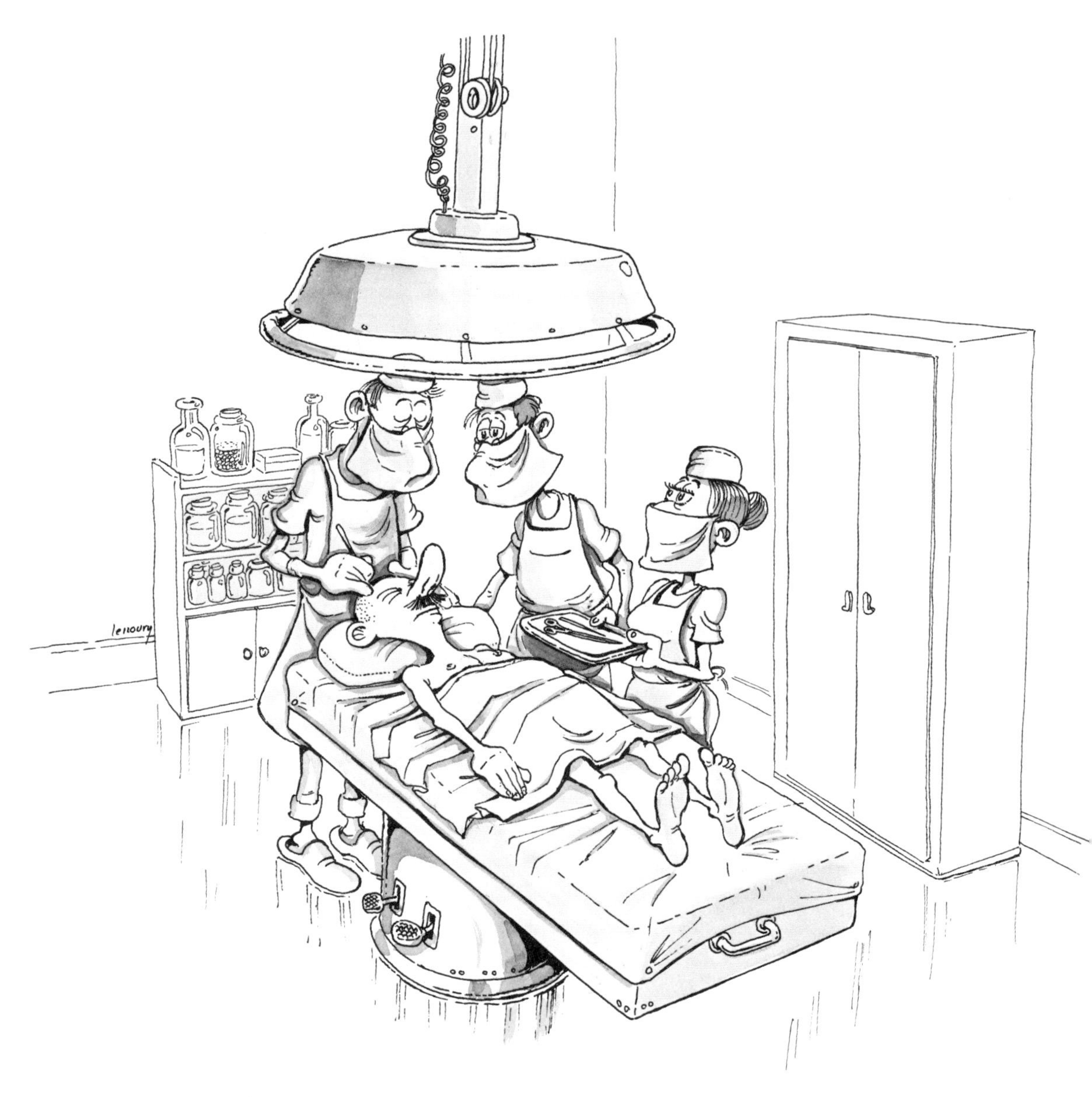

This is it!? No panel screws? No circuit boards? . . .

lenoury

This time I'm debugging it for keeps!

Sorry, Pop—your computer's too primitive for my homework.

Three billion to one against being rescued—Thank God for the computer or we'd never have known!

It says: He won't make it through the night—demand payment in full.

It tries that on everyone. Let it know who's boss!

lenoury

Crush your ego! Shatter the illusion of reality! Purge the dream of earthly pleasure. Half an hour with our computer billing program should do it . . .

Look, ***you*** *tell Big Foot we don't have Pac-Man! . . .*

Sorry about your raise, Langer, but the computer just won't approve it.

Goddam those computerized dashboard readouts! . . .

COMPUTERS RUN EVERYTHING HERE.

lenoury

Let's face it, the computer designed the house perfectly . . . well, almost . . .

lenoury

lenoury

Yeah, I know it can do calculus, analyze the spiritual state of any given person according to the laws of Karma, predict next weekend's weather in the Bahamas, compose a symphony in any key for any combination of instruments, translate 783 languages and dialects from Arabic to Zulu, pass judgment on a legal brief in light of the Moldavian constitution of 1735, control the air conditioning of an open-pit mine, investigate any piece of information or run any project on the planet—but ***what'll it do for me?***

Which one of you guys controls Times Square?!

I sought happiness in success, money, love, religion—then I found it in nature, in the simple life. I grow my own food, I make my own clothes—my computers do the rest.

Ooops!

Run? Waddaya mean run! If it ran would I be debugging it?

50 percent of 100? Just a sec, I'll check it . . .

SHIFT
RETURN

It says that if we remove one eye, both hands, both feet, and both ears you'll be perfectly normal.

. . . and this is the programmer's office . . .

NOT TONIGHT,
DEAR,
I HAVE A
HEADACHE.
PORNO
lenoury

Maybe we better dump the computer and get the chef back . . .

Send us thy manna, Oh Lord!

Sure, his computer's terrific, but our hardware can match it.

This town's not big enough for both of us! . . .

Best we can do 'till the computer network's hooked up.

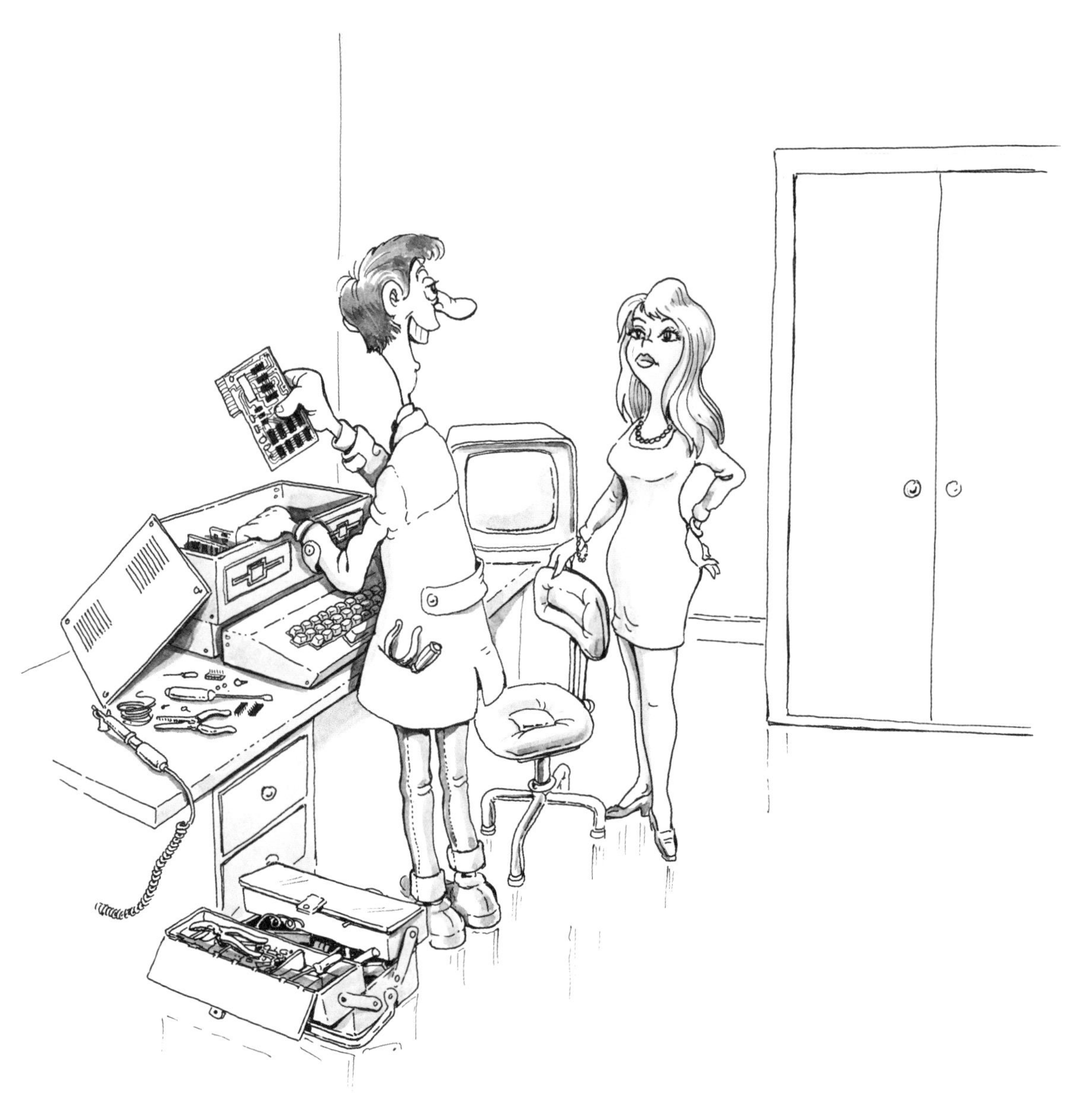

Come on up to my place, honey—I'll show you my applied interfacing techniques.

You sure about this new computerized aiming system, Jones?

They say it all started with a bug in a computer program . . .

Finally made a big breakthrough in communicating with the damn thing.

CTRL SHIFT RETURN BREAK INSERT CLEAR GOTO
SELECT START ≤ DELETE BAKS ← SHIFT LOCK
SYSTEM RESET ↑ RETURN LINE FEED ESC RPT
SHIFT ↓ RETURN BS → SELECT INSERT +
ENTER SHIFT 1 = CTRL START= RETURN + ≥ , 0
CLEAR BACKSPACE TAB PRINT REM . . . .

N°
34781
lenoury

lenoury

Plug in the computer and ask it where the lamp plug goes . . .

Sorry, your employment profile is not what we're looking for.

*But is the world **ready** for computerized architecture?*

You say your computer can replace my secretary . . .

Sorry, boss, we were playing with the video game and it took me all night to escape from the maze.

First call an ambulance. Then find a volunteer to tell him that for the past three hours he's been entering data into a broken memory bank . . .

COMPUTER
ROOM

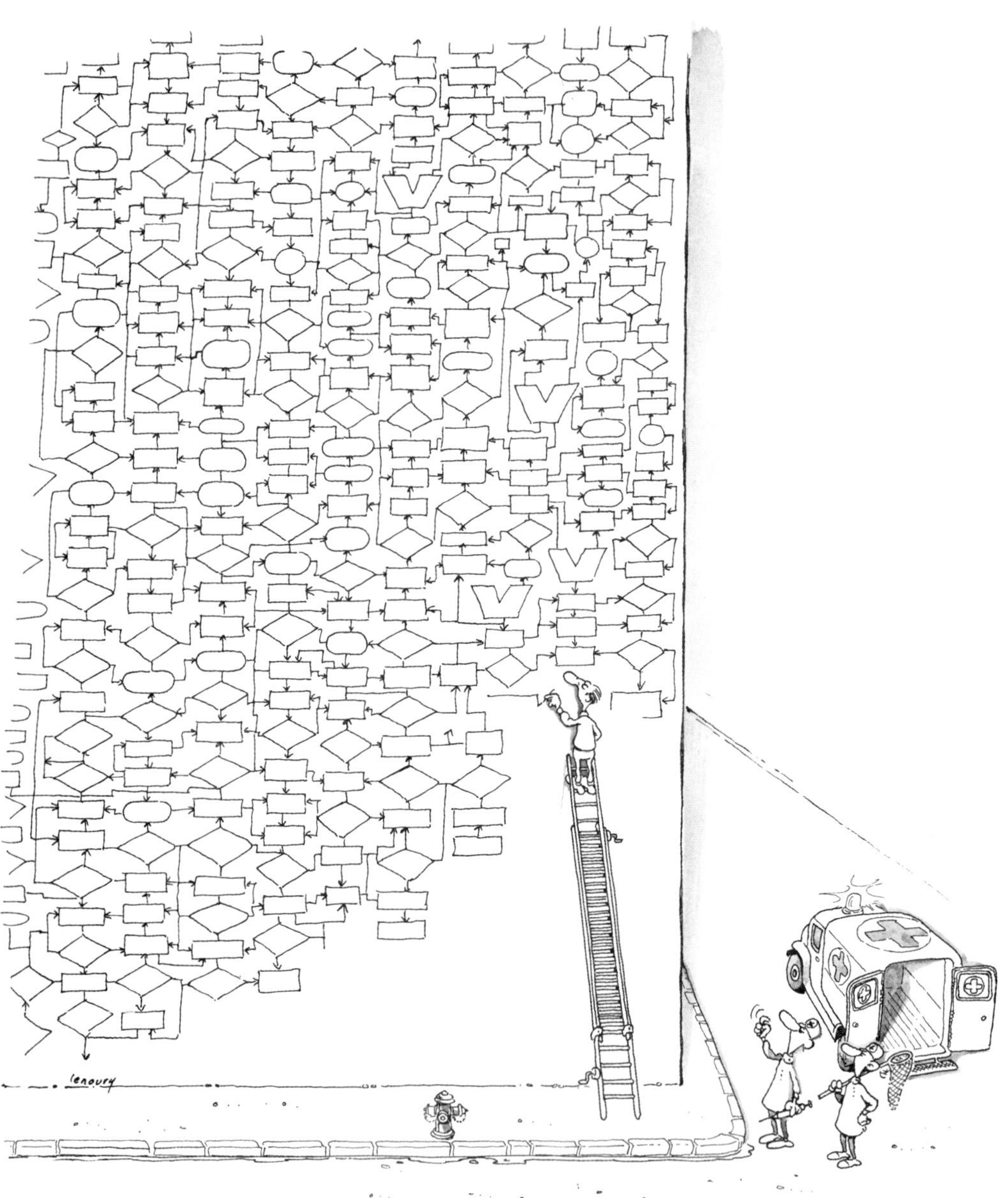
lenoury

E=MC²
lenoury

But the computer dating service described someone a bit—um—different . . .

Look, I'm not taking any crap from you this morning!

Finally found some use for the damned thing!

lenoury

Congratulations on that great computer setup, Terwilliger—
which, by the way, has just replaced you.

I've programmed it to fetch my slippers and paper, but I can't get it to stop wetting the rug.

It's been a lot more cooperative since I told it that its life hangs by a wire.

DON'T DISTURB
SHIFT
CTRL
A
E
X
lenoury

Computer crazy?

SYBEX can make things a lot easier for you. We publish an entire line of computer books, including humor and children's books, introductions to computing, buyer's and user's guides, and technical books. Let SYBEX be your personal computer expert. Ask about our books wherever computer books or computers are sold, or send for our catalog.

SYBEX Inc.

For a complete catalog of our publications please contact:

U.S.A.
SYBEX, Inc.
2344 Sixth Street
Berkeley,
California 94710
Tel: (800) 227-2346
(415) 848-8233
Telex: 336311

FRANCE
SYBEX
6-8 Impasse du Curé
75018 Paris
France
Tel: 01/203-9595
Telex: 211801

GERMANY
SYBEX-Verlag GmbH
Vogelsanger Weg 111
4000 Düsseldorf 30
West Germany
Tel: 0211/626441
Telex: 8588163

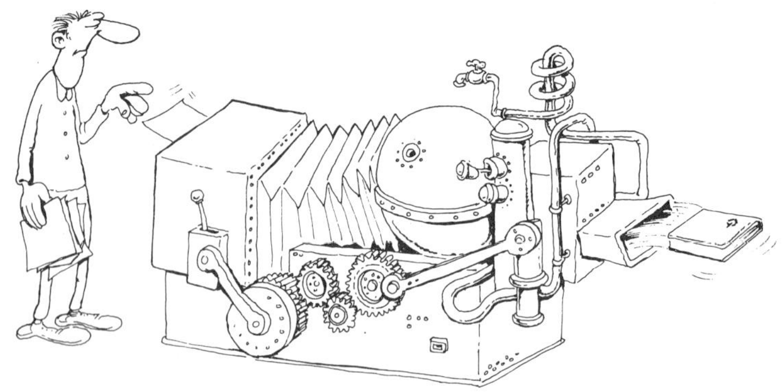